Smartphone

Help

Contents

Introduction

Welcome to a short but useful resource for Android smartphone maintenance and optimization!

In today's fast-paced world, smartphones have become a ubiquitous necessity, helping us stay connected, informed, and entertained. Android devices especially smartphones have become the ubiquitous necessity of today but they come with a fair share of glitches and errors. The fuming user, who has in most cases spent a huge sum on the phone, is generally clueless about how to fix the phone. Mostly smart phone fixers take advantage of this naivety of users and charge high rates of fixing glitches, leading to user discomfort and anxiety.

This simple guide will help you learn the basics of smartphone maintenance. We'll cover the basic maintenance tasks that every Android smartphone user should know, including cleaning your phone, freeing up storage space, and optimizing battery life. We'll also dive into troubleshooting common issues such as slow performance, overheating, and unresponsive screens, and provide you with step-by-step instructions for resolving them. Additionally, we'll share essential security and privacy tips to help you keep your personal information safe from prying eyes.

Whether you're a tech-savvy enthusiast or a non-techie looking to take care of your Android smartphone, this book has got you covered. With our easy-to-follow instructions and expert guidance, you'll learn how to keep your phone in top shape and get the most out of your investment. So let's dive in and discover the secrets of Android smartphone maintenance and optimization.

The good news is that with the right maintenance tasks and optimization tips, you can keep your phone running smoothly and securely for years to come.

We wish your <u>android device</u> a happier, healthier, and longer life!

The battery not charging!

Keep your Android Battery Alive! Don't batter it!

Lithium-Ion batteries are commonly used in android smartphones, tablets, and other portable electronic devices as they are lightweight and have many performance benefits. Despite their main advantage of the lowest self-discharge among all the available batteries, lithium-ion batteries begin to wear out because of the continuous charging and discharging cycle of the smartphone. An older battery will not hold the same charge as a new one.

To slow down this wearing-out process and extend battery life, some pointers should be kept in mind:

Don't let the android battery be fully discharged before charging it!

Try to charge your battery before it is finished to prevent damage. If you let your battery go all the way to 0 (empty), you will be shortening its lifespan drastically (more than half).

For this purpose, keep a portable charger (e.g. a car mobile charger) available readily so that the phone can be saved from discharging completely and hence powering off. The following table shows that completely discharging the battery decreases its no. of discharge cycles, thus lowering the overall battery life.

100% discharged	300 – 500 discharge cycles
50% discharged	1,200 – 1,500 discharge cycles

No overheating your android

Heat causes a lot of damage to lithium-ion batteries used in <u>android phones</u>. Do not put your phone in direct sunlight or near a heat source like the stove. Even keeping it in temperatures above 40 degrees Celsius can cause permanent damage to your battery. Permanent capacity loss is speeded up by high temperatures. Using android applications while the phone is charging can also cause overheating. The cooler the phone remains when not in use, the higher its performance standard and hence lower battery consumption. Therefore, smartphone users who expose their phones to high temperatures or carelessly place their phones in the sunlight often complain about their batteries being discharged all of a sudden.

Loss of capacity per year at 0°C -> 6%

Loss of capacity per year at 25°C->20%

Loss of capacity per year at 40 DEGREES CELCIUS-> 35% capacity loss

To Prevent overheating:

1. Close unused apps: Running too many apps in the background can cause your phone to overheat. Make sure to close any unused apps by going to your phone's recent apps and swiping them away.

2. Check for updates: Outdated software can cause your phone to overheat. Make sure to check for any available updates for your phone's operating system and install them.

3. Turn off unnecessary features: Features like Bluetooth, GPS, and Wi-Fi can also contribute to your phone overheating. If you're not using them, turn them off.

4. Remove phone case: A phone case can trap heat and prevent your phone from cooling down. Remove your phone case and see if that helps with the overheating issue.

5. Check for rogue apps: Some apps can cause your phone to overheat. Check for any apps that might be using too much processing power and causing your phone to overheat. To do this, go to your phone's settings, then to "Battery" and check which apps are consuming the most battery.

6. Keep your phone out of direct sunlight: Sunlight can also cause your phone to overheat. Keep your phone in a shaded area or indoors if possible.

7. Restart your phone: Restarting your phone can sometimes help with overheating issues. Turn your phone off and on again and see if that helps with the problem.

Do not overcharge your phone battery

Try to unplug your charger before the battery is completely charged. This could potentially overheat the phone, although some android phones stop charging automatically once the battery is full. Most android phones also display an instruction message about unplugging the charger once the battery is full. The battery aging process is accelerated by frequently charging it to a full hundred percent. Mostly, phone users keep the charger plugged into the phone and forget to unplug it once the charging is done, leading to overcharging and hence damaging the battery permanently.

While the Android device is charging, try not to use it.

A novel fact about lithium-ion batteries in android phones is that using the phone when it is still charging can damage the battery. This usage is generally harmful because it prevents the battery from entering a full charge cycle. Nowadays, it is a common practice to keep using the phone while charging, sending texts, or making phone calls is not halted even for the scarce time during which the battery is being charged, leading to permanent damage. Smartphone addiction has led to permanent battery damage because the gadget is not granted rest even during the process of charging the battery.

Battery drain :

Battery drain is a common issue that many smartphone users face. Here are some steps you can take to troubleshoot this issue:

1.   Check battery usage: Go to your phone's settings and check the battery usage. This will show you which apps are using the most battery. If you notice any app using an unusually high amount of battery, consider uninstalling or disabling it.

2. Turn off unnecessary features: Turn off features like Bluetooth, Wi-Fi, and GPS when you're not using them. These features consume a lot of battery, even when they're not in use.

3. Adjust screen brightness: Lowering the screen brightness can help save battery life. You can also enable the adaptive brightness feature, which automatically adjusts the screen brightness based on ambient light.

4. Use battery-saving mode: Most Android smartphones come with a battery-saving mode that reduces the phone's performance to save battery. Enable this mode when your phone's battery is low.

Turn Off functions you are not using

Data services take up a lot of battery time. Most of the time you will not be using these services yet they will still be draining your battery. Turn off GPS, Bluetooth even Wi-Fi if you are do not require them. According to a survey, 78% smart phone users keep their Wi-Fi service switched on even when they are not using it because they get a 'sense of connectivity' through it. They think switching off their Wi-Fi would disconnect them from the general world. This is the main reason of battery drainage in Android phones these days. When the Wi-Fi is unknowingly kept switched on, the phone keeps working on application updates and downloading extra files, leading to faster battery drainage.

Power saving mode

Use power saving mode whenever possible. Lower the brightness to save battery power. Remember to delete apps you are not going to use. Battery is also drained out when the phone vibrates upon receiving a phone call or text. Unless otherwise required, do not use the vibration feature of the phone as it drains battery rapidly.

Cleaning

Cleaning Your Smartphone: To clean your smartphone, you'll need a microfiber cloth, a soft-bristled brush, and some rubbing alcohol or a cleaning solution specifically designed for electronics. Start by turning off your device and removing any cases or covers. Then, use the brush to gently remove any dust or debris from the surface of your device. Next, apply a small amount of cleaning solution to the microfiber cloth and use it to wipe down your device, taking care to avoid any openings or ports.

Finally, let your device air dry before turning it back on and replacing any cases or covers.

Charging Carefully

In some cases lint gets into the socket where the charger connects in the android phone. Clean it carefully with a pin if you have trouble charging. Also be sure to use a genuine charger rather than a fake one. Staunch phone users mostly connect fake or borrowed chargers to charge their phones temporarily, which is detrimental to the phone's battery in the long run. It is better not to charge your android in extremely warm, humid conditions or around water. Wireless chargers also add to the amount of heat produced in the android phone. Chargers should be placed in clean and moderate temperature environment when not in use, as it affects their efficiency.

Connectivity Issues

If you're having trouble connecting to Wi-Fi or Bluetooth, try turning off and on the connectivity feature or restarting your device. If that doesn't work, try forgetting the network or device and re-adding it. If the issue persists, check for any available software updates for your device or try resetting your network settings.

Always remember the Memory issues

Even a brand new android phone can bother you with messages like "low memory" when you try to install unwanted and space consuming apps. This is because the internal memory becomes full rather quickly, after all the internal memory comes packed with preinstalled apps. Also all apps use the internal memory of your android first as well as RAM (temporary memory for faster access) rather than the micro SD card which generally has more space compared to the other two types of memories on your phone(internal memory and RAM). Sometimes, the phone keeps on running applications at the back end without the user knowing it, which continue consuming battery silently, discharging the phone fast. Therefore all the data should be stored on SD card, and all the unwanted applications should be shut down.

In order to free up android's internal memory, the user can:

Delete unwanted applications.

Clear application caches

Clear all sort of browsing history

Disable immovable applications and move installed applications to your SD card.

Store media files such as pictures, mp3 files, music, videos etc. to the external memory, usually the SD card.

Crashes and Freezes

If your phone is freezing or crashing, try a soft reset first by holding down the power button until the device restarts. If the problem persists, try clearing the cache of individual apps or the entire system cache.

To clear the cache of an app, go to

Settings > Apps > [App Name] > Storage > Clear Cache.

To clear the system cache, turn off your device, then hold down the volume up button and power button simultaneously until the recovery menu appears. Use the volume keys to navigate to "Wipe cache partition" and press the power button to select it. Once it's complete, select "Reboot system now".

If the issue still persists, you may need to factory reset your phone. Make sure to backup your data before proceeding. To factory reset your phone, go to Settings > System > Advanced > Reset options > Erase all data (factory reset) > Reset phone.

Smart phones are not like desktop computers, rather their processing slows down or in some cases hinders completely, if multiple apps are kept running at a single time. Therefore to maximize a smart phone efficiency, it is suggested that unwanted apps should be closed and reopened when required. Nowadays, background task killer software are also available for the ease and facility of the user, which keep deleting background applications on a regular basis.

Delete unwanted apps

Warning: DO NOT uninstall system apps as it could corrupt your phone! Delete only those apps that you do not need.

It is a common misunderstanding that deleting default apps would fasten the phone and improve the phone's performance. However it is not true, rather the phone might start malfunctioning if default apps are deleted. The standard procedure for deleting unwanted applications is:

Go to Settings

Then select Applications or Apps

Then select Manage Apps

Delete apps you are not using

Generally android doesn't let you uninstall preloaded apps. Nevertheless these apps can be "disabled" and as a result they will stop updating or running in the background.

Slow phone :

Slow Phone Performance

If your phone is running slowly, try freeing up storage space by uninstalling unnecessary apps and deleting old files. You can also try clearing the cache and data of individual apps to free up space.

Freeing Up Storage Space: To free up storage space on your smartphone, start by reviewing the files and apps you have installed. Go through your photos, videos, and music to see if there are any duplicates or files you no longer need. You can also use the storage settings on your device to see which apps are taking up the most space and delete any that you don't use. Additionally, you can move files and apps to an external SD card or use cloud storage services to store your data.

To clear the cache and data of an app, go to Settings > Apps > [App Name] > Storage > Clear Cache/Clear Data.

Another way to speed up your phone is to disable or limit animations in the Developer options. To access Developer options, go to Settings > About Phone > Software Information > Build Number (tap it seven times to activate Developer options).

From the Developer options menu, scroll down to the "Drawing" section and change the following settings: Window animation scale, Transition animation scale, and Animator duration scale. You can either disable them or reduce the animation duration to speed up your phone.

Clear all sorts of browsing history:

Mostly users are unaware of the fact that whenever a webpage is opened and surfed on a smart phone, its path remains saved in the browser's history. In this way, pages keep on getting accumulated in the history section of the phone's browser, making it slow and occupying the memory storage. To solve this problem, it is important to delete browser history almost daily or every other day. An even more effective way is to check the option in the history section of the browser which says 'delete history daily' so as to make the browser efficient on its own.

Clear app cache:

A cache and history log is made when the internet is used or apps are run or downloaded. The purpose of cache is to store data of an App or website to make loading faster. However as cache takes up your phone's precious memory, it slows the android down and can cause problems with the functioning of other applications, and in most cases, functioning of the phone as a whole.

1. Go to "Settings" on your Android phone.

2. Scroll down and tap on "Storage" or "Storage and memory."

3. Tap on "Internal storage" or "Phone storage."

4.   Tap on "Cached data" to clear the cache.

5.   Confirm that you want to clear the cache by tapping "OK."

When the cache is deleted, so are the settings that go with it. It will be as new. You will have to login again.

To clear your cache for an individual "misbehaving" app:

Go to Settings and tap on Application Manager

Tap on the "misbehaving" app

Now you will see the details of that app

Click on clear cache to remove the cache

Gesture Navigation: To use gesture navigation on your Android device, swipe up from the bottom of the screen to access the home screen. Swipe up and hold to see recent apps, or swipe from either side of the screen to go back. To access settings, swipe down from the top of the screen and tap the gear icon.

Night Mode: To enable night mode on your Android device, go to Settings > Display > Night Mode. From here, you can turn it on and off, schedule it to turn on and off automatically, and adjust the color temperature and intensity to your liking.

Do Not Disturb: To enable Do Not Disturb mode on your Android device, swipe down from the top of the screen to access the Quick Settings panel, and tap on the Do Not Disturb icon. From here, you can choose to turn it on immediately or schedule it for a specific time. You can also customize it to allow certain notifications through while muting others.

Digital Wellbeing: To access Digital Wellbeing on your Android device, go to Settings > Digital Wellbeing. Here, you can see how much time you spend on your device, set app timers to limit your usage, and enable features like Wind Down, which turns your screen to grayscale at night to help you wind down before bed.

Device Maintenance: To use device maintenance on your Android device, go to Settings > Device care. From here, you can run a quick or full scan to check for software updates, battery optimization, and storage optimization. You can also clear out junk files, and enable auto optimization to keep your device running smoothly.

Factory resetting of the phone

It's better to factory reset the smart phone if it gets really clogged up, though it's not always a viable option. This means that the phone might need restarting and shutting down every hour or so. This is because some bugs and viruses can only be eliminated completely if the smart phone is factory reset and phone is refreshed from the grass root level. **Only an expert can factory reset your smartphone! Do not attempt to do this yourself**.

Screen the Screen- Physical protection of your Android

Your android phone is a valuable investment. Protecting it from damage is very important. Preventing damage is easier and cheaper than fixing the damage once it's done. The more you take care of your device, the longer it functions efficiently.

Unresponsive Screen

If your phone's screen is not responding, it can be frustrating. Here's what you can do to troubleshoot this issue:

1.   Restart your phone: Press and hold the power button until the power menu appears. Tap on the "Restart" option to restart your phone.

2.   Remove the case: If you're using a phone case, remove it and see if the screen starts responding.

Sometimes, cases can interfere with the phone's touchscreen.

3. Clean the screen: If your screen is dirty or covered in smudges, it may not respond properly to touch. Clean the screen with a microfiber cloth to remove any dirt or smudges.

4. Calibrate the screen: Some Android smartphones come with a screen calibration feature. Go to your phone's settings and look for the "Display" option. From there, you can calibrate the screen to improve touch response.

Location
One has to be careful about where the phone is placed. Don't put your phone in dangerous places like:

The edge of high places

In the reach of children and pets,

Near water –or in the rain

Near a heat source

Definitely in the reach of babies and toddlers, as all they do is chew the phone!

Use a case for your Android

Using a case helps in protecting your android from damage in case of falls and water contact.

You also need a screen protector and not just a case. Scratches on your screen will ruin your experience with the android phone. Scratches can come from sand- (which is why you should be careful on the beach), rocks, jewelry, watches etc. scratches not only destroy the look of your phone, but also hinder the ultimate touch experience of your gadget, as screen touch sensor is highly sensitive.

Security

Keeping Your Phone Safe and Secure:

1. Install antivirus software: Use reputable antivirus software to protect your phone from malware, viruses, and other online threats. Some popular options include Avast Mobile Security, Norton Mobile Security, and McAfee Mobile Security.

2.   Keep your phone's operating system and apps up to date: Regularly update your phone's operating system and apps to ensure that any security vulnerabilities are patched. You can check for updates by going to "Settings" > "System" > "Software update."

3.   Use a strong password or passcode: Set a strong password or passcode to secure your phone. Avoid using common or easily guessed passwords like "1234" or "password." Instead, use a combination of letters, numbers, and symbols.

4.   Avoid downloading apps from third-party app stores or untrusted sources: Stick to downloading apps from the Google Play Store, which scans apps for malware and other security threats. Avoid downloading apps from

third-party app stores or untrusted sources, as these apps may contain malware or be designed to steal your personal information.

5.   Enable two-factor authentication: Two-factor authentication adds an extra layer of security to your accounts by requiring a second factor of authentication, such as a code sent to your phone or a biometric scan. Enable two-factor authentication for your accounts whenever possible to reduce the risk of unauthorized access. You can enable two-factor authentication for apps like Google, Facebook, and Twitter in their respective settings.

Keeping your phone safe and secure is essential. Smart phones are basically small computers and are equally susceptible to viruses, malware and spyware. You should install an antivirus app to scan your phone. This will slow down your phone but you can always uninstall it later. However, anti-viruses are also of many categories, and only authentic and effective antivirus should be installed.

Locking the phone

You should lock your phone with a password, PIN or pattern. This could keep a person from physically accessing your phone, especially in case it's dropped, lost or stolen. For this first go to settings then tap personal security and then select screen lock. Automatic screen lock is also effective in this case; the user can always auto lock his phone by changing settings. Nowadays, thumb impression technique is also an innovation and protection rate is the highest if one has this feature in one's phone.

Download apps only from trusted sources

Some apps might affect the device's security, so it is recommended that the user should download them only from trusted sources. Google play and play store are deemed the safest in this regard, as they pass the apps through stringent policy checks, including checks for potentially harmful behavior. Therefore, installing apps from unknown sources is surely a risk for the smart phone.

Always be careful about ads

Mostly ads on unknown random websites are gateways to viruses and spam installation in your smart phone. Social networking websites like Face book and twitter have a multitude of ads being placed on them as well as being played from different sources. Therefore, when such websites are accessed, it is deemed mandatory to delete browsing history, delete caches and all the downloaded data from the browser on a regular basis.

Conclusion:

Though smart phones are no less than blessings in the eventful world of today, their maintenance and protection is an immense concern for their users. Smart phones not only entail physical protection and covering, but also require regular software updating and maintenance. Taking care of the battery and recharging it aptly is a needed practice most users are unaware of. A healthy battery maintains a healthy smart phone. Simultaneously keeping track of the phone's memory and checking on its usage is also the utmost need of every gadget. Appropriate memory usage surely leads to a longer and more durable life of the smart phone in hand. A smart phone is a personal device, the more secure, the better. It needs secure and protected applications for its optimum usage. Exposing the phone to unsafe and malicious software and apps might decrease its resilience and quality of performance. Therefore, it is the need of the hour to take care of your smart phone, because it can benefit you to an optimal extent only if it is healthy and well preserved.